D1414684

DISCARD

Artist's Studio

Singing

by Jenny Fretland VanVoorst

Bullfrog Books

Ideas for Parents and Teachers

Bullfrog Books let children practice reading informational text at the earliest reading levels. Repetition, familiar words, and photo labels support early readers.

Before Reading

- Discuss the cover photo. What does it tell them?

- Look at the picture glossary together. Read and discuss the words.

Read the Book

- "Walk" through the book and look at the photos. Let the child ask questions. Point out the photo labels.

- Read the book to the child, or have him or her read independently.

After Reading

- Prompt the child to think more. Ask: Do you like to sing? Have you ever sung with other people? Did you enjoy it?

Bullfrog Books are published by Jump!
5357 Penn Avenue South
Minneapolis, MN 55419
www.jumplibrary.com

Library of Congress Cataloging-in-Publication Data

Fretland VanVoorst, Jenny, 1972– author.
  Singing / by Jenny Fretland VanVoorst.
    pages cm. — (Artist's studio)
  Includes index.
  ISBN 978-1-62031-285-8 (hardcover: alk. paper) —
  ISBN 978-1-62496-345-2 (ebook)
  1. Singing—Instruction and study—Juvenile. I. Title.
  MT898.F74 2015
  783'.043—dc23
                                            2015021768

Series Designer: Ellen Huber
Book Designer: Michelle Sonnek
Photo Researcher: Michelle Sonnek

Photo Credits: All photos by Shutterstock except: Alamy, 20–21; Dreamstime, 16–17; Glow Images, 4, 5, 6–7, 8–9, 11; pio3/Shutterstock.com, 16–17; SuperStock, 12, 14–15, 19; Thinkstock, 22br.

Printed in the United States of America at Corporate Graphics in North Mankato, Minnesota.

Table of Contents

Vocal Studio

Tom is a singer.

He sings in a choir.

Tom has a deep voice.
He sings the lowest part.

His voice blends with the others.

Some voices are high. Some are low.

Together they make a rich, full sound.

Imagine you can hear them.
Listen!

How do they sound?

Deb is a singer, too.

She writes
her own songs.

She plays guitar.

Her voice is high.

It is clear.

She sings in coffee shops.
She sings in the
subway, too.

Imagine you can hear her. Listen!

18

How does she sound?

Try it yourself!
Singing is fun!

Inside the Vocal Studio

guitar

conductor

microphone

sheet music

Picture Glossary

blend
To mix thoroughly so that the things mixed cannot be recognized.

imagine
To form a mental impression of something.

choir
An organized group of singers.

subway
A usually electric underground railway.

Index

To Learn More

Learning more is as easy as 1, 2, 3.

1) Go to www.factsurfer.com

2) Enter "singing" into the search box.

3) Click the "Surf" button to see a list of websites.

With factsurfer.com, finding more information is just a click away.

24